A New Ecosystem

for Sustaining Children

© 2018 Clean Law

Family Law 2.0: Hatching a Superstate...

International Standard Book Number: **978-0-9975507-7-1**

1. Profession 2. Family 3. Law 4. Policy
5. Science

Printed in the United States of America
with United States Constitution jurisprudence.

Clean Law
is green law
www.cleanlawunion.com

CONTENTS

Forward 15

Introduction. 19

Thorny Fences

1. Farming Other Fields 23

Good Farming With Child Sustainability Crossings

2. The Contemporary Parent/Child Sustainer 29

3. The Eye of the Adult Fighting File Storm. 33

4. *#ResetFamilyLaw* 37

5. The Represented Child Safety File Life 43

6. The Most Fragile in Divisive Deals 49

7. Why Can't Family Law See Child Vulnerability? 55

8. Family Law 2.0. 59

9. Reuniting Your Parenting 63

Child Sustainability Systems are Sprouting

10. What's Science Doing About It?. 73

11. The Superbridge 77

Incubating Child Safety Systems

12. Double Family Law 87

13. The Safety File. 93

14. The Superstate – Next-Generation Safety. 99

15. Conclusion 103

Accelerating Family Law 2.0

16. Children's Bill of Rights 109

17. Fertilizer – *The Fair Deal Standards Bill.* 115

Acknowledgements. 121

Fresh New Seeds of

Love & Prosperity

Calibrated for Child Safety

SYSTEMS —

ARE THEY DYING OR THINKING?

The answer is yes.

Family Law 2.0 is about two different types of law practices and how each one effects our states differently. This book creates a villain called the void monster based on true shortcomings in classical family law. It creates Bridge heroes who dug in deep for the cause of a new scientific foundation. A sacrificial lead of putting children first that was necessary for turning a supervoid into a superstate. The thesis of Family Law 2.0 was to expose the shortcomings of the single family law practice along with the benefits of a double family law 2.0. A Theory which seamlessly includes a state-of-the-art scientific law practice beginning with child safety files. May God bless the USA.

Void monsters are everywhere in Illinois. Many of us can remember the first disconnected void monster that we were ordered into. The ole "deadbeat" label for being laid off of work or in an accident and not able to work. And that's exactly how many truly innocent parents are being treated by single law levers today. Children have no right to counsel. Parents have nor right to counsel when they can't afford it. Comply with lever "law," or else be pressed into it with voidness until you cave. Many truly innocent parents dream of being treated as well as criminals.

People in most states love nothing more than to abuse their power. The rule s are, either think like they think. Or else you and especially your children can and will be placed in an inescapable void. That is a fact.

The real victims are the real victims. It's a nightmare watching innocent parents drop like flies in these void monsters while justice for real victims is compromised. Innocent parents in family court are created to stand in these open voids underneath waterfalls of false opposing accusations. That's one giant void monster.

The financial voids over decades of abuse are off of the chain. Being verbally persecuted is one thing. But being pencil whipped on a report by an authority figure is a completely other thing. Being taxed multiple times as hard as you fight against it is a drowning thing sometimes worse than water boarding. This creates voids in every part of your life. Financially, socially, professionally, and in time with children. If you're in a car accident and comma, then you may be in violation of child support, a deadbeat, worth pencil whipped, and not worth representing. Your life might be down the drain.

So the challenge is, how do we as united parents break free from those spirals of void monsters in classical family law? At least for our children's sake?

The answer is by pitching a reality based "double law," hatching a superstate, incubating child safety files, and accelerating micro justice. This Family Law 2.0.

CHILDREN ARE

ALWAYS FRAGILE

Introduction

Children are in everything.

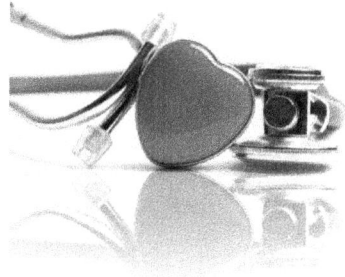

Children grow up to become
everything from doctors to
nurses, to teachers and reporters.

Children are precious and essential.

So, it's vital that we do the very best that
we can for next generation safety.

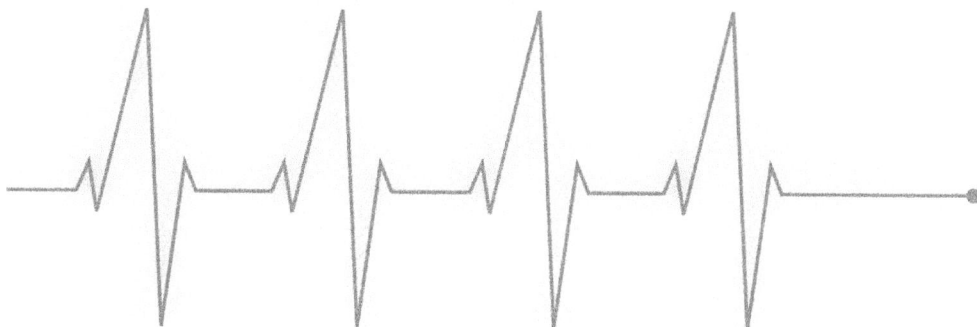

Thorny Fences

1. Farming Other fields

Ya know it never fails. City folks 'round here always judge me for farming other fields. It's not that the grass is always greener on the other side. It's just that when you go through a decade or two of old family law while wanting to raise your own crops in your own field, then guess what by golly? That's exactly what's illegal! You're programmed not to farm in your own field. You're programmed to farm other fields!

Now I'm no prim and proper suit and tie worker like those city slickers. I'm just a farmer. We say that a suit is why Spiderman can't grow a garden. But if I can't farm my field, then I'm no good.

I often sit in an old rocking chair outside on the front porch wondering what could have been. I feel the cool breeze on my neck and face as I rock back and forth listening to the combines workin far away. During those crisp evenings of fall harvest there's a smell of dust in the air. A hankerin' to get out there and do something productive. But city people just don't understand how dangerous that is.

My ole 1992 John Deere 9500 combine sure could've cut a lot of wheat back in its prime. But then it got ordered to stay in the shed and wasn't allowed to farm in its field ever again. Oh, it tried one time back in '93. But it got caught. And as punishment a brand new shiny motor guard was taken away. That guard was in tip-top shape I tell ya. I used to wax and polish that thing every year. The sun would shine off it like a crystal when we drove it down the road. But it was just taken off and thrown in the dump like trash for trying to do what it was meant to do. It was like here's a spoon for your good and healthy bowl of soup. But if you eat it, then we're going to take it away. Oh, those crops look so-o-o appealing. But what's a farmer to do?

Another time I felt like I wasn't being a good farmer and noticed that some weeds were growing in my new field of wheat. So I climbed in the combine, pulled it out of the shed, and drove down the road to near where the weeds were growing in the field. I cautiously looked around before I stepped out of the cab and climbed down the ladder. I turned and took a couple of steps and then a giant leap to get across the ditch between the road and the field. Climbing up the embankment and sneaking into the field, I felt like I was doing the right thing trying to cut those weeds down. But dag-nab-it the neighbor saw me! And then that neighbor told another neighbor. And then the word got around. And by the time it got back to town Godzilla must've been out in that field stompin kids to death. The story was that I drove right through door of the shed and flew down road like a drunk mad man to the field and then jumped the ditch like Evil Knievel and was doing donuts out in the field like Dale Earnhardt. By then, it was way too late to find out what really happened. The suits didn't need a trial to come out and flatten all four tires. I guess I should've known better than to try and farm my own field.

Before long, other damages to my combine became the routine. Metal guards on the auger were dented after I tried to harvest. Gears where taken off and thrown into the dump. Then sugar was put into the fuel tank. The rims got bent. I just could not figure out why trying to farm plants that I helped plant in the landlord's field was so bad.

Some of us country folks know things that city folks don't know. Things that people who haven't experienced it would never believe it in a million years. There's something wrong with trying to save our own wheat kernels in our own fields from being turned into chafe. Outside combines can literally come in and turn our wheat to chafe but we can't farm our own fields and save the wheat.

So, I guess I can farm other fields and eventually work my way back to my field. And why not? That's what I am programmed to do. Old family law never lets us grow our own crops.

Today, I only try to farm other fields. It's like why wash my own windows when that's dangerous and it's safer to wash other windows? Other farmers can come in and go out of my field freely. Other combines can come and go as they please. But I can only farm other fields with an old broken-down wobbly combine. What a gig! And what a waste of gas! Those city slickers have no idea what they're doing. The old family law principle is that children of divorce can be around anyone else in the whole wide world except their own parents. And it doesn't matter if a parent is the best parent in the world or the worse parent in the world. A child of old family law can legally be around a mass murderer but not their own parents. That's not justice. Heck, that's not even American! The old family law "run a rumor cause it always sticks" mill minus justice is why combine owners like me can only farm other fields. Those stinkin' thorny fences. They're an ecosystem for devastating children!

Good Farming With

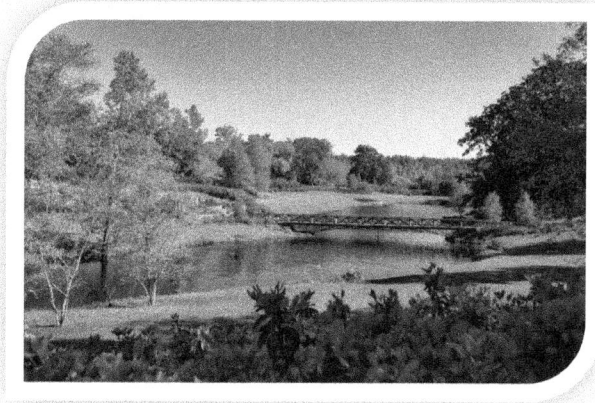

Child Sustainability Crossings

2. The Contemporary Parent/Child Sustainer

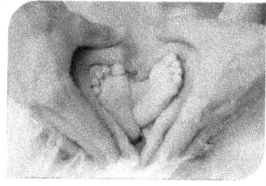

The Contemporary Parents Code

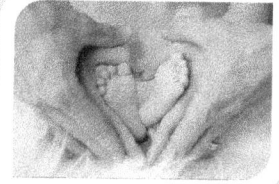

...the greatest of these is love.

Throughout divorce and separation,
    dad and mom are in strict competition.
That's the world we live in,
    and no one else is to blame.

So what would the world look like,
    if we start keeping score of the kids?
What will divorce and politics look like,
    when we code in the kids?

Throughout Cardinals versus Cubs,
    teams are in opposition.
That's the world we live in,
    and no one else is to blame.

But what would Decatur be like,
    if we kept score of the kids?
What will Decatur look like,
    when we rezone the kids?

Throughout Plaintiff versus Defendant,
    teams are in competition.
That's the world we live in,
    and no one else is to blame.

But what would America be like,
    if we kept score of the kids?
What will America be like,
    when we rezone the kids?

Throughout Democrats versus Republicans,
    teams are in strict competition.
That's the world we live in,
    and no one else is to blame.

But what will the world be like,
    if we kept score of the kids?
What will the world be like,
    when contemporary parents code in the kids?

Contemporary Parents – Authors of encouraging safety files, family law 2.0, and future policies for children of conflict.

Faith ♥ hope ♥ love ♥ value ♥ positivity ♥ encouraging evidence ♥ safety throughout mean divisive worlds

3. The Eye of the Adult fighting File Storm

When mom and dad go on a trip,
    but a child stays home,
with no one to advise or monitor,
    then void monster, what's your function?

When parents are warring apart through family law,
    but no team feels the pulse of a child,
then void monster, what's your function?
    Are you meant to drain the community?

When there's a left pen and a right pen,
    but no pen for a child,
then void monster, what's your function?
    Are you meant to drain the city?

When there's a Plaintiff party and a Defendant party,
    but no party for a child,
then void vampire, what's your function?
    Are you meant to drain the county?

When there's left case law and a right case law,
    but no logical case law for a child,
then void supervampire, what's your function?
    Are you meant to superdrain the state?

When Aron's freedom to talk to his daughter was blocked,
    and Alayna's phone separation was locked,
then void monster, what's your function?
    Are you meant to drain the community?

When Chris' trial went on and on,
    and Madison's separation was fair game,
then void monster, what's your function?
    Are you meant to drain the community?

When Denis had a dream of the right to bail,
    and Evan's separation was the deal,
then void monster, what's your function?
    Are you meant to drain the community?

When Wemple dreamed of a right to counsel,
    and his children disappeared instead,
then void monster dumpster, what's your function?
    Are you meant to drain the community?

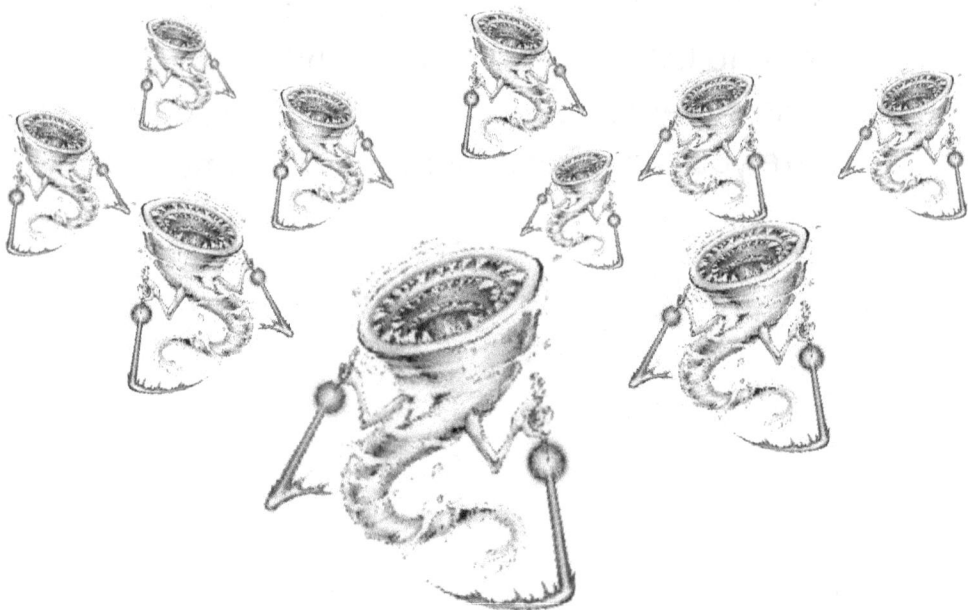

4. #FamilyLawReset

CUSTODIAL **"VERSUS"** **NON-CUSTODIALS**

Parents slave names: One step-up/lump, or two steps-up/lumps, or three, or four, or more forevermore???

Yah. We all get it. You're child's an outcast to classical family law. Principles overly excluded non-custodial parents and overly include custodial parents. Teachers overly excluded non-custodial parents and overly include custodial parents. All representatives alike overly excluded non-custodial parents and overly include custodial parents. Yah. We all get it.

Yah. We all get it. Some are casts. Created to come in first. Meant to always be looking ahead. Yah. We all get it.

We all get it. We're outcasts. Created to be left out. Meant to be always looking over our shoulders. Yah. We all get it.

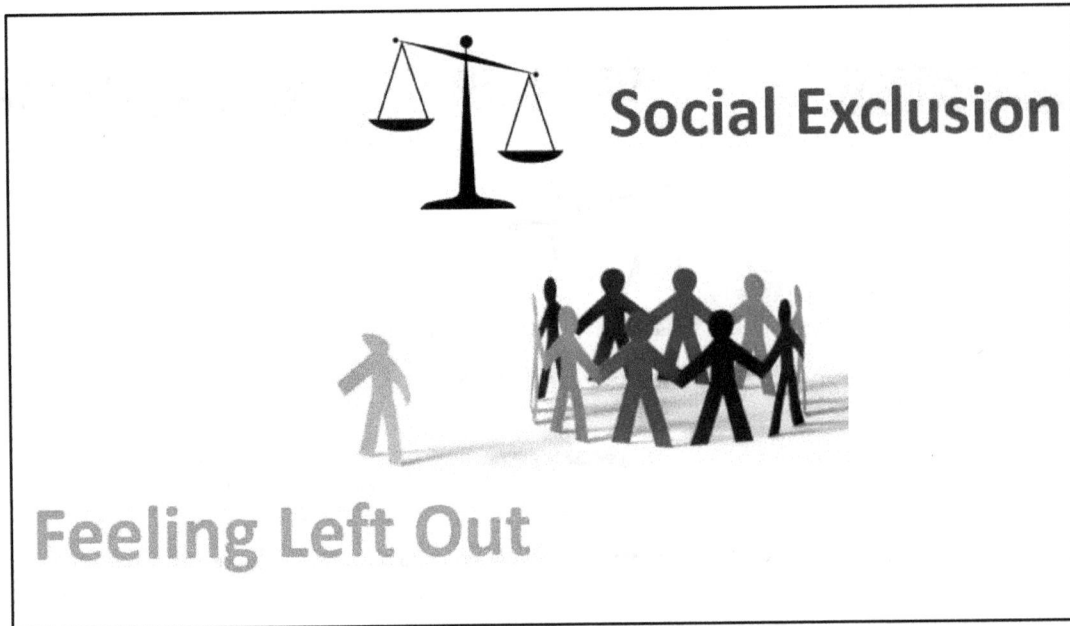

Social Exclusion

Feeling Left Out

Ya. We all get it. Classical family law grows us delusioned. Superior "versus" inferior is the rule. Custodian "versus" non-custodian parent labels inequality forever. And those involved but who are left out (the children) feel it the most.

Contemporary Parent and/or Contemporary Parent

Parents Freedom Names: One fair chance at your idea or issue, or two fair chances, or three, or more forevermore???

Yah. We all get it. Family Law 2.0 grows sanity, equality, and child inclusion up tall. And Contemporary Parents are doing this seamlessly.

Why not both seamlessly?

#ResetFamilyLaw

Social Inclusion

Feeling Included

#ResetFamilyLaw

5. The Represented Child Safety File Life

When mom and dad go on a trip,
    and a child stays home,
but with a connected monitor and advisor,
    then Contemporary Parents, what's your function?

When parents are warring apart through family law,
    and safety files inflate to catch child,
then CLU Contemporary Parents, what's your function?
    Are you meant to conserve the community?

When there's a left pen and a right pen,
    and now a pen for the child,
then CLU, what's your function?
    Are you meant to conserve the city?

When there's a Plaintiff party and a Defendant party,
    and now there's a party for the kids,
then CLU bridge, what's your function?
    Are you meant to conserve the county?

When there's left case law and right case law,
    and now logical case law for a child,
then CLU superbridge, what's your function?
    Are you meant to superconserve the state?

When Aron dreamed to talk to his daughter with freedom,
    and now there's Alayna's Law to pick that lock,
then CLU, what's your function?
    Are you meant to conserve the community?

When Chris' trial went on and on,
    and now there's Madison's Initiative,
then CLU, what's your function?
    Are you meant to conserve the community?

When Denis had no right to bail,
    and now there's Evan's Initiative,
then CLU, what's your function?
    Are you meant to conserve the community?

When Wemple had no right to counsel,
    and now there's Christian's Law,
then CLU fountain, what's your function?
    Are you meant to conserve tomorrow's community?

Voids beget voids,
        Bridges beget bridges,

Void monsters beget
        void monsters,
Clean Law begets
        clean law,

Void monster vampires beget
        void monster vampires,
Clean Law fountains beget
        cleaned law fountains,

Void monster supervampires beget
        void monster supervampires,
Clean Law superfountains beget
        clean law superfountains.

Cleaning up monsters together
        regardless of our differences,
Glues America back together
        no matter how big our ditches.

Clean Law
is green law
www.cleanlawunion.com

6. The Most Fragile in Divisive Deals

"What you can measure you can manage."

— Peter Drucker

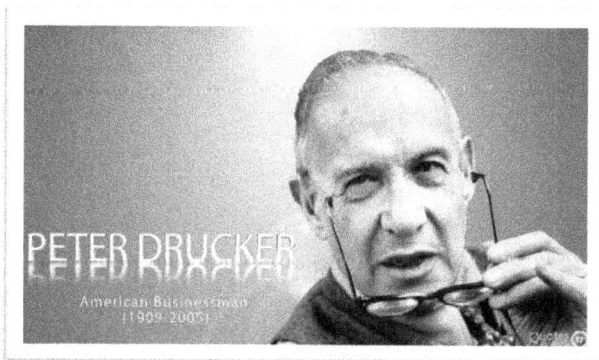

Peter Drucker is described as
"the founder of modern management"

Accounting for Lost Sight, Lost Sound & Lost Value of a Child After the Split-up of Parents

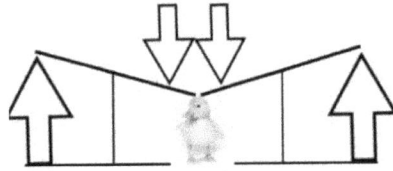

After a divorce or separation, children customarily loose 20% of the sight, sound and value of their custodial parent, and 80% of the sight, sound and value of their non-custodial parent. And children of classical family law loose 100% of the sight, sound and value of both of their parents together. These Lost Sight, Sound & Value Accounts deduct more from children than they do from adults. And the harder that the break-ups are, then the more counter leverage these children feel. Family law is not fair to chilldren.

With children in school, the respective sight, sound & value losses per year are estimated below.

	Custodial Parent:	Non-custodial Parent:	Child or Children:
1 year	-665 hrs	-2,662 hrs	-3,328 hrs
5 years	-3,325 hrs	-13,310 hrs	-16,640 hrs
10 years	-6,650 hrs	-26,620hrs	**-33,280** hrs

WARNING:

The heaviest loss with the closest family is on children.
Children are the most vulnerable after a split-up.

Without Safety Files

Other Accounts where Children Lose More than Adults after a Divorce or Separation:

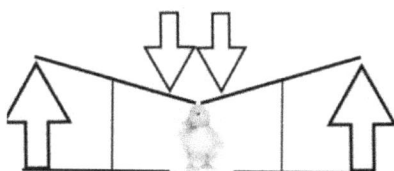

- ❖ **Sense of Normalcy**
- ❖ **Love, Joy, Peace, Happiness**
- ❖ **Typical Touch, Taste, Smell**
- ❖ **Financial**
- ❖ **Family**
- ❖ **Friends**
- ❖ **Etc.**

WARNING:

"Superunfair!"

Without Safety Files

Single family "law" versus "law" pens.
Classical family law is a void monster to the entire family.

7. Why Can't Family Law See Child vulnerability?

Below are the Top 10 Voids in the classical "fighting files" of divorce court which prohibits the classical law practice from seeing the split-up child abuse. (Because of these voids, the classical law practice cannot address the unfairness that children of divorce court suffer from).

Classical "Fighting Files" (the need to fill)

"Layers and years of downward momentum"

The Top 10 Voids in the fighting files of divorce court that hide falling children:

1. The Versus Void (as in mom <u>versus</u> dad)

2. The Table-less Void (as in <u>no</u> table in court)

3. The No Voice Void (as in <u>no</u> equal voice)

4. The No Representation Void

5. The Intelligence Gaps

6. The Misplaced in Contracts Void (listed with property)

7. The Hidden Rules Firewall

8. No Statistics

9. No Research and no Studies

10. The Party-less Gap (as in Plaintiff, Defendant, etc.)

SAVE ME!

Dangerous For Kids

Without Safety Files

<u>Bridge heroes</u>:

Aaron Wemple and Chris Clark fell so deep in old family law that they wound up in a homeless shelter together. Aaron's case was over, but Chris' case was still pending. That must've been a divine appointment.

Chris was going through a case and thought that his daughter Madison was lost in the trenches because he just received notice that his parenting rights were being restricted. Which is kind of understandable giving the situation. But not without a legal fight and some kind of due process to hear the facts in the case. But unfortunately, no matter how hard Chris tried, that day, like Aaron's, would never come. Proof that the void monster does exist.

Denis Durham had a dream. He dreamed that every child subject to family law would have a bill of rights like patients at the hospital where he worked. Because without rights, false accusations bounced their dad back and forth between systems like well-oil machines. Proof that the void monster exists and is getting hungrier.

Aron Buttram had a dream. Criminals have the right to counsel but parents in family law only dream about. The unrepresented life of Aron Buttram constantly saw his phone time with his daughter regulated against and interfered with. A unique void monster which proves they do exist.

Sandy Ashley has a dream of reuniting children and grandchildren like her own. The unrepresented life when she was younger gave her the experience to know how easy it is to lose children. And how challenging it can be to reunite. Her unique void monster which proves they do exist in classical family law.

Charlie Friend has a dream of keeping bridges clean and free of muck. Sure he works at the Department of Transportation. But he's seen how easy it is for roads to get dirty when they're never maintained. Now, this may not sound like a dream team for family law 2.0. But what did ya' expect? United parents who have never been in a trial?

8. Family Law 2.0

Everyone always asks, "What is CLU?" Or, "What is this Clean Law Union?" And I guess the short answer is that CLU is to family law what new software is to a computer. United parenting is an updated version of family law. Or, family law 2.0.

We're not saying that anything is wrong with classical family law. However, it should have at least been properly maintained. You don't buy a 1936 Chevy Coupe and just let it sit and rust out in the weather at best. Or, at worse put it in an acid bath of a similar rusting factory. You maintain it to keep it operating properly. Likewise with the original version of family law and every case that just sits there in the clerks office idle.

Old family law is like an old motorcycle which doesn't run and sits out behind the shed. Or, like a 1984 computer that doesn't work and isn't compatible with anything.

The long answer is that CLU is family law 2.0 and is set to be released December 26, 2018 as a gift to the world in honor of Lord Jesus who makes it all possible. CLU is like a brand new motorcycled parked in the garage. Or, like a brand new smartphone.

CLU is updating and improving family law and even customized family law for particular cases. You see, reuniting with children isn't just a border issue. Many American parents need help reuniting with their children. It's not too bad to re-connect a telephone line or a cable service when they are disconnected. But re-connecting with children of a high conflict divisive divorce requires expensive legal services at best. Like buying car or putting a down payment on a house. At worse, it's just a drain and a practice of futility. Like being in a sinking ship and putting more holes in it the harder you try to stay afloat.

CLU was designed for parents who cannot afford an attorney. Unlike criminal law, family law has no right to counsel when parents cannot afford it. Parents in a divorce were typically left holding the bag weather they asked for the divorce or not. They were left paying again when that system failed them, or when its old mechanisms did not jive with life. They were left holding the bag to find understanding of what happened and even trauma recovery. And the children of old family law were paying the heaviest price. Many teachers said that they could recognize children of divorce. So CLU researches each case from a scientific law perspective and initiatives new legislations or deregulations in honor of those children who paid the price for next generation safety. CLU is customizable family law 2.0.

Future family law is going to be more like accurate surgery and less like an inaccurate mud throwing contest, or mud packing events. Family law 2.0 is like what a child safety seat inside of a Tesla state-of-the-art luxury car is to the automotive industry. And less like what an injured duckling is to alligators in a swamps

CLU is a new industry improving family law. It's a safety bridge, prayer/research center & family trial support group for divorce court and other trials all in one. **"Bridges for Families!"**

9. Reuniting your Parenting

REUNITING *Your* PARENTING

SUPERVOID ALERT

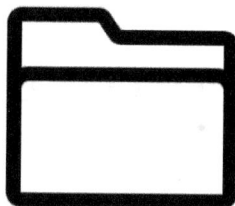

Reunite
CLU BRIDGE

SUPERVOID ALERT

What is it?

In family law trials, there are 10 major structural voids and many minor voids in that mechanical system that children are falling through. That's the supervoid.

How does this happen?

The classical law practice, or "single law," that's currently being used in family court is not scientific. It is mechanistic. Which means that it has no senses to see, hear, or value the supervoid. Just like it has no way to see, hear, or value children.

What can help?

1 - Child Safety Files

2 - Contemporary Parents

3 - Family Law 2.0

4 - Policies that build bridges

5 - The Fair Dealing Standards Bill

Like police & DCFS who interview children, "safety files" can bridge the old family law voids to finally see, hear, and value the children of divorce and high-conflict policy making.

The "Double Family Law" Theory says that as Family Law 2.0 increases, then crime, poverty & injustices will decrease.

CLU BRIDGE

POSITIVE
PARENTAL RIGHTS
www.cleanlawunion.com

THE SUPERVOID CHALLENGE

*If anyone believes that supervoids in fighting files and fighting policies are safe, then take the **Supervoid Challenge**. Be the unseen, the unheard, unvalued, unrepresented, party-less term of two opposing fighting parties. You will learn where you stand. And that falling is your manifested destiny. Farming other fields to survive while that's illegal too.*

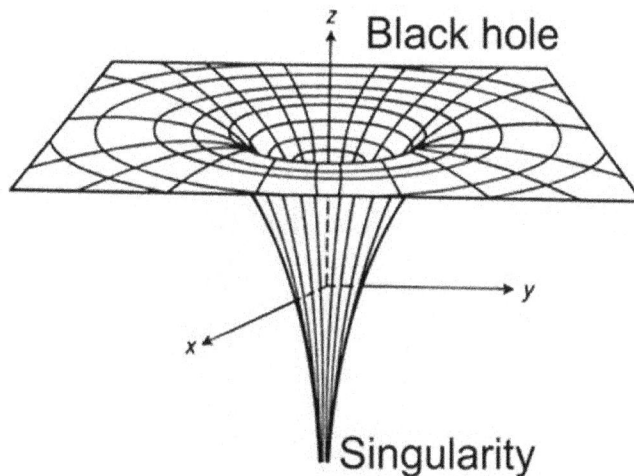

You'll feel left out and bound forever worse than a criminal.

THE SUPERVOID

"Life" In Illinois

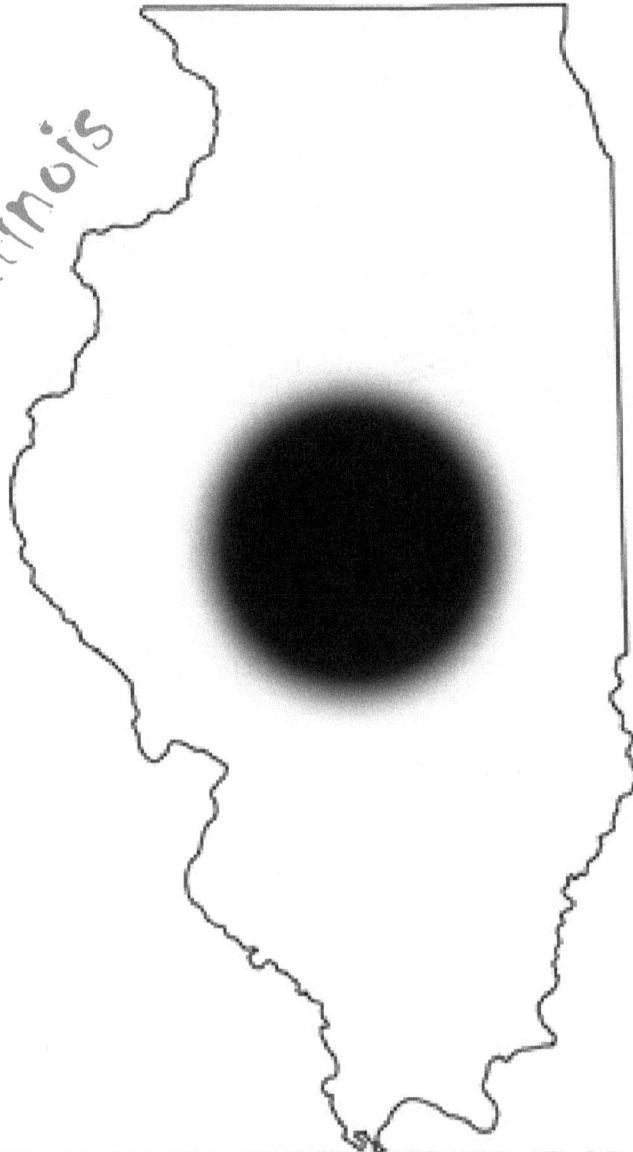

Where the void steals your heart and eats it too.

CLASSICAL "LAW" LEVERAGE VS. "LAW" LEVERAGE

"FALL LAW"

ONLY | ONLY

LOOK OVER THERE!

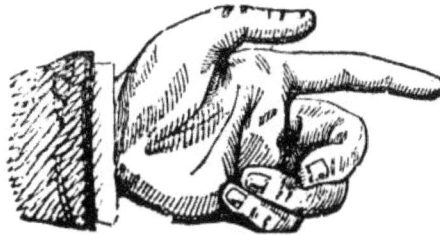

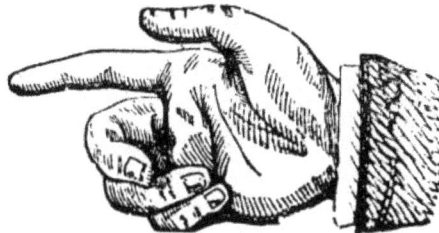

Fooled You, Didn't We?

LOOK OVER THERE!

Fooled You, Didn't We?

R.I.P.

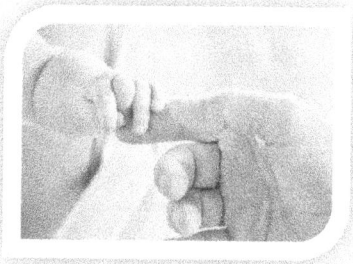

Child Sustainability Systems are Sprouting

10. What's Science doing About it?

What can science do?

✓ Science can monitor and manage losses.

✓ Safety files use scientific law.

✓ Scientific law is inherently constructive in all ways.

✓ Scientific law is perfect for building children of family court up.

✓ Safety can help those treated unfairly

✓ A breakthrough in child safety.

Code Kids In!

With Safety Files

Classical family law, unfortunately, segregates children at the border of "custodial" and "non-custodial" labels. Which is also demeaning and dehumanizing.

Family law 2.0 integrates children with "mother" and "father" labels that creates inherent meaning and humanization.

Old family law voids and mechanisms resemble a layered labyrinth of ins and outs and ups and downs with plenty of unpublished "pass" or "fail" labels separating the chosen ones from the unchosen ones. If an unfavored child is not chosen, then it's beyond expensive to be free from the layered labyrinth of classical family law. Which obviously is inherently also very dangerous.

Void monsters like continuing a case beyond reason. Continuances are just one example of a void, but they're often used recklessly without so much as feeling the pulse of the children involved. And mechanistic steps separate the rich who can afford an attorney who knows those steps from the poor who cannot those who know those steps.

(Source: https://steemkr.com)

Some say that the balance of power is left side or right side of the scale. But a true balance of power is lifting the bottom up. It's natural. A true balance of power integrates these littlest children who were left out. And the true a balance of power puts them above their own careers.

That's what CLU's family law 2.0 has routinely accomplished. And all for free. Lifting up those who can't even get in the door to be on the radar of decision making is family law 2.0. The beginning of child safety files for next-generation safety above the voids and mechanisms from classical family law.

11. The Superbridge

AARON WEMPLE'S SUPERSTATE THEORY:

SCIENTIFIC LAW IS NOT COMPATIBLE WITH FAMILY LAW,
BUT THEY CAN BE INTEGRATED TOGETHER SEAMLESSLY WITH
CHILD SAFETY FILES AUTHORED BY CONTEMPORARY PARENTS
CREATING A STATE-OF-THE-ART SUPERSTATE.

Spring Law

<u>"The Other Law"</u>

What do politician's have in common with constructive engineer's scientific law?

In a real world, why not real law too?

Is the world ready for
Double Family Law?

Double Family Law
is designed to hatch
maximum child safety,
incubate superstates,
and to accelerate micro justice for all.

"CONNECTION
is
ENERGY
that the disconnected will never see."

– Aaron W. Wemple

INVENTIONLAUNCH
NEXT GENERATION SAFETY

"SINGLE LAW" - PROTECTION

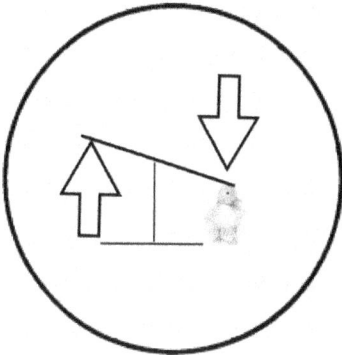

Child abuse is like a bully taking advantage of the differences between inflatable strengths and deflatable weaknesses. A visualization of that dynamic is this picture where the left side of a scale is inflatable in every conceivable way while the right side of the scale is dependent and deflated in every counter "conceivable" way. Victims of child abuse are fortunately surrounded by protective files at the Child 1st Center, DCFS, police, the state's attorney, and other wonderful organizations. "Single law" files protect **after the fact.**

"DOUBLE LAW" – NEW CHILD SAFETY

Void pains feel like a jackhammer tied to both of your wrists and making you hit your own head. In family court, opposing sides counter the other side and can't see what the middle feels until it's too late. Void pains can last for years when the system is overplayed. But now, fortunately, there's a new invention for child safety. Safety files prevent children of family court from void pains. "Double law" relieves **during the fact**.

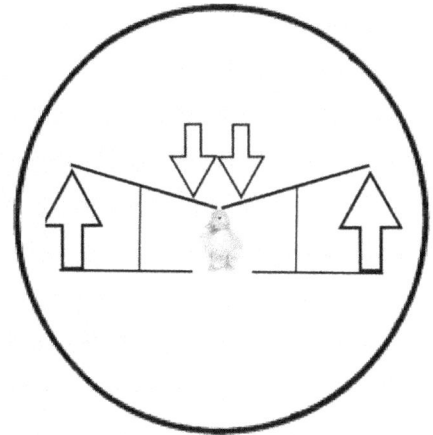

THE FUTURE IS PREVENTION

Safety Files can **prevent void pains** that the classical family law void monsters can't even see. The littlest people can now feel safe, seen, heard, represented, and valued by the authors of their lives during trials and before impactful decisions. Because of common disconnects, safety files work for children in family court, for students who are bullied, and for children who are tricked out of their parent's life. "Double Family law" prevents pain **before the fact**!

SUPERBRIDGE

Theoretically, child safety files would grade the unfairly treated children by how well they are handling it (a divorce or parental plit-up), what helps, and what hurts worse. This supervoid safety would be like getting graded at school.

Children who are being supervoided out of classical "fighting files" could feel seen, heard, and valued with child safety files.

INVENTION LAUNCH

Code Kids In!

With Safety Files

Incubating Child Safety Systems

12. Double Family Law

Without Safety Files

With Safety Files

Code
Kids In!

Double Family Law: *Child safety files from a scientific law (constructive) perspective alongside fighting files from a courtroom law (deconstructive) perspective will save lives, help students, and improve our community.*

We put bicycle lanes next to car lanes, child car seats next to adult car seats, and even happy meals next to value meals. And children are always fragile. So, why not offer state-of-the-art safety files with classical fighting files?

Without Safety Files

Code Kids In!

With Safety Files

Double Family Law is Needed

     In Macon County, Illinois Case Number 16-D-401, Aron Buttram and his daughter Alayna had become puppets on the strings of fighting file inconsistencies. Not everyone can afford an attorney. And the right to counsel is not the same for criminal law as it is family law. In this case, legal filings transitioned from a physical system to an electronic filing system. Unfortunately, the other parent in this case worked at the courthouse. And Aron's efilings became like a bug zapper keeping justice away. As you can see from the before and pictures of the online courthouse docket sheet, inconstancies are rampant. Yet, victims will never know it unless they know to watch it and to take before and after screen shots of the circuit clerks docket sheet after you do a file search.

     Fortunately, double family law was just coming online in Decatur, Illinois. Aron signed up and became a proud contemporary parent. And together, files where cleaned and Alayna was a little safer from the void monster.

Without Safety Files

Code Kids In!

With Safety Files

04/19/18	Plaintiff personally present.
04/19/18	Defendant personally present.
04/19/18	Plaintiff objects to the Petition for Modification of Child Support.
04/19/18	Parties directed to file financial affidavits by 5/4/18 and proposed calculations by 5/11/18.
04/19/18	Cause continued for hearing on the Petition for Modification of Child Support.
04/19/18	Petition/modify set for 05/25/2018 at 1:30 in courtroom 5B.
04/19/18	---------------------------------------

Void

No defense recorded by the clerk in court on the docket sheet for the Defendant, but witnesses present have Affidavit's that the Defendant asked not allow Plaintiff's "48 day" Response to his Petition because it violated Illinois Supreme Court rule 902.

Before

05/03/18	----------------------------------
05/03/18	Financial Affidavit with Proof of Service filed by JANKOWICZ, JAMES.
05/03/18	----------------------------------

After

05/03/18	----------------------------------
05/03/18	Financial Affidavit (Aron E Buttram) with Proof of Service filed by ARON BUTTRAM.
05/03/18	
05/03/18	----------------------------------

The back side only of this filing was email to the Defendant to mail to the Plaintiff and her attorney after it was efiled correctly. This voids the legal step required by law.

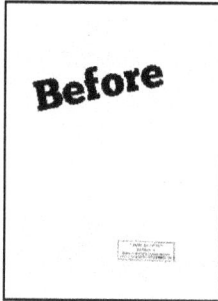

Before

The page was hand-given to the Defendant by a clerk the next day after debate and routine constant revolving tries.

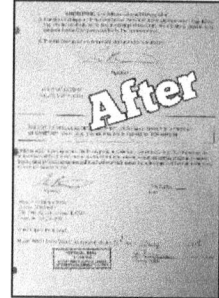

After

07/03/18	----------------------------------
07/03/18	Petition for Rule to Show Cause filed by JANKOWICZ, JAMES.
07/03/18	----------------------------------
	Notice for Rule to Show Cause filed by JANKOWICZ, JAMES.
07/03/18	----------------------------------
07/03/18	Agreed Parenting Plan filed by JANKOWICZ, JAMES.
07/03/18	

Before

07/03/18	----------------------------------
07/03/18	Petition for Rule to Show Cause filed by Butram , Aron
07/03/18	----------------------------------
07/03/18	Notice for Rule to Show Cause filed by Butram, Aron
07/03/18	----------------------------------
07/03/18	Agreed Parenting Plan filed by Butram, Aron
07/03/18	----------------------------------

After

Changing a name on the docket sheet and emailing filings backwards may not seem like a big deal. It's like applying for a credit card and giving you your card with someone else's name on it. It can't be used. Not to mention that it creates a void in victim's mind and jeopardizes the child involved. Victims are defrauded out of whatever is one the line in these revolving punitive actions. And without safety files, perpetrators often claim that the victim is mentally ill. No one believes a common person over a county employee. Sometimes the victims are even tucked away nicely into a mental institution and never heard from again, or never credible enough again to question these punitive actions against them in old family law fighting files.

Without Safety Files

With Safety Files

Code Kids In!

13. The Safety File

SAFETY FILES (filling the need)

"Next Generation Safety"

1. Void 1 Safety (Private file in child's name)
2. Void 2 Safety Bridge (Exclusive table)
3. Void 3 Safety (Give children a voice)
4. Void 4 Safety Bridge (Contemporary Parent)
5. Void 5 Safety (Connects intelligence differences)
6. Void 6 Safety (places children correctly in deals)
7. A New Path (Consolation at the "no rules" Wall)
8. Statistics
9. Research & Studies
10. #Unity is the new Party!

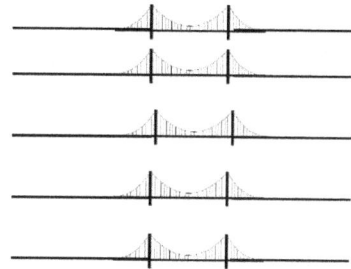

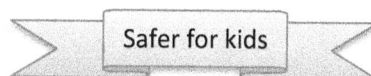

Wow! Maybe I'm not supposed to fall?

Safer for kids

A few people might have worries about privacy in child safety files. However, no vital information like social security number is needed. And the scientific law practice is inherently constructive. It documents only the positives. Not the negatives. Plus, it's children's own Contemporary Parents authoring these files.

This inherent support and encouraging system is also something that everyone would like to share. After all, if an author wrote a book about you from a most flattering perspective, then wouldn't you be okay with that? That's how safety files work.

For example, if one attorney continued a case for months and months to try and gain an advantage of the other side who may not be able to afford it, then a safety file would document the great things that happened in the child's life during that time to try and offset that void monster.

Safety files could comfort children during the roughest conflicts in their lives. Just think, perhaps someday there will be no more trauma, or life-long post-trauma from high conflict divorces. That nightmare won't have to haunt these children for the rest of their lives with child safety files. Prisons would be thinner and homicides would be reduced. Drug addictions and early teen pregnancies could finally be reduced. Escapes from the severe childhood trauma of divorce would no longer be need with the child integrations of a safety file.

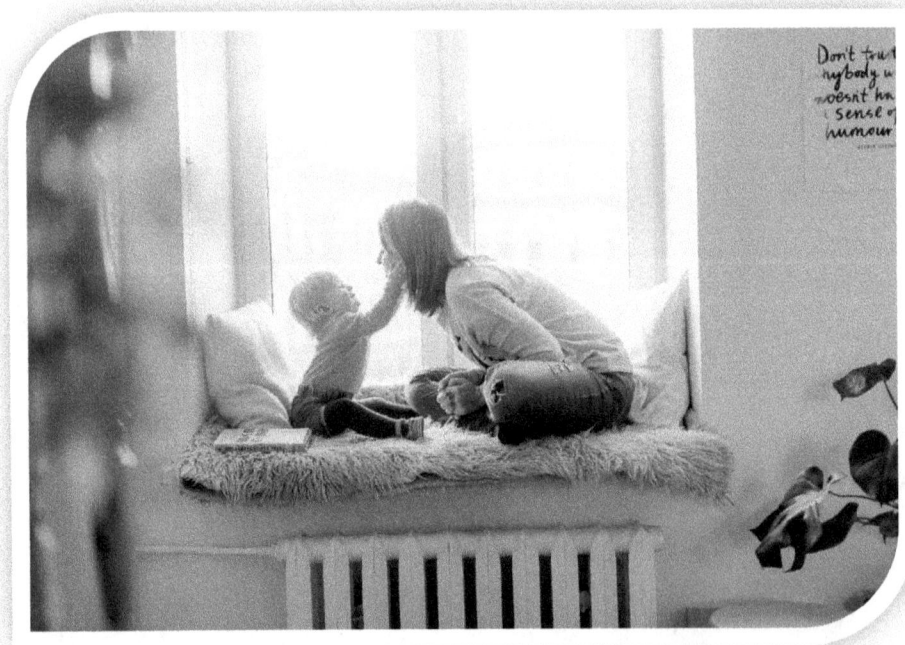

SAFETYFILESINCUBATION
NEXT GENERATION SAFETY

By Aaron Wemple d/b/a Clean Law Publishing

Drought. That's the current forecast for any baby Uncle Sam in divorce court.

Farmers in Central Illinois know how to grow good corn in all types of circumstances and environments. But what about kids? Do you know why leaders do not know how to grow good children of conflict? Because they're falling through the cracks of divorce court like grain falling through the cracks at the grain elevator.

When safety files begin following children through the divorce court "fighting files" mechanisms, like following a kernel of corn through the grain elevator, then more eyes will be on them, more ears can hear what's best and worse for them, and more value can be given to them.

Farmers keep track of seeds, storage, pre-processing, hatching plants, incubating weather, harmful circumstances, accelerating conditions, decelerating conditions, and post-processing.

Safety files now keep track of children, storage, and divorce court processing. Monitoring this human elevator of mechanical steps, family law clerks, and family lawyers, we'll be able to track in between pre-processing and post-processing to know how to best relieve the drought of divorce for these fragile children. We learn in Biology that plants need a photoperiod amount of time in the sun. But children also have a psyche. Do they need a parentperiod amount of time with each parent to be healthy?

This safety file pilot program by CLU in Decatur, IL is a volunteer effort to improve system safety for families and community wellness. Free plug & play safety files learn, publishes and will consistently grow good children of high conflict divisive divorce. Which is an ever-increasing need.

Today, no one knows if any one way or another is better for growing the children of divorce court. A famous quote by *Dr. Brené Brown says that "Connection is the energy created when people feel seen, heard and valued."* Are children of divorce court growing up without energy? How big is their drought?

Tomorrow, these children will be caring parents who should know more about growing good children of divorce. And CLU is free. So, nothing legal can stand in the way. We can and should learn more for them.

The people who convey cases through family court and those who decide how much child support there is, can't see what baby Uncle Sam's favorite food is. Or, what allergies baby Uncle Sam may have. They can't hear what baby Sam's favorite comfort word is. Or, what word scares baby Uncle Sam and why. And they can't grade how well or how bad baby Uncle Sam endured a divorce. Life for baby Uncle Sam is a drought.

If we're trying to do what's right to build a functioning Ford Model T on an assembly line, but never see a bolt placed on a nut, hear a motor run, or grade a tire, then can we ever really do what's in the best interest of a Model T? If we try to grow a healthy plant, but never look at the seed, hear the wind, or grade the soil, then can we ever grow a good plant? Can court ever really tell us when to tighten a wheel or water a plant?

Since classical family law clerks and family lawyers never see, hear or value children of low, medium or high conflict divorce, then can we ever really do what's in the best interest of these children? Or is low, medium and high undocumented droughts the only path for them that can be taken?

What if all vehicle nuts and bolts were built perfectly tight like vehicles at Caterpillar? What if all seeds were able to grow within specified environments like ADM farmers? What if all children of high conflict divorce were unwiltable like at CLU? Would crime decrease? Would a more civilized society increase?

What if we could slowly and seamlessly turn Illinois into a superstate?

We put bike lanes next to car lanes, child car seats next to adult car seats, and even Happy Meals next to Value Meals. So, why no child safety files next to divorce court fighting files?

What would the world be like if the forecast for children of family court was good for growing?

14. The Superstate –

Next-Generation Safety

✓ Estimated Pain Relief from the Top 10 Voids:

✓ Children will feel safer during splits on the order of 10 times

✓ 10 times Void Pain Relief over 10 years = 100 times pain relief!

✓ Children of family court alone with a safety file (Resiliency Plan) could very well have a healthier future!

The New CLU

"Union Parenting Yes"

Badges
For
Bridges

Family Law Stop-gaps

cleanlawunion.com

15. Conclusion

Family Law is antiquated. Millennials in family law deserve a safer future.

With next generation safety, kids in Family Law 2.0 can grow up to be healthier in everything. Children can be better doctors and nurses, better teachers and reporters. After all, children are the most essential ingredient to progress.

Passion creates motivation, which leads to innovation

Craig Groeschel

Clean Law
is green law
www.cleanlawunion.com

Accelerating Family Law 2.0

INTEGRATING CHILDREN

with

CHILD SAFETY FILES

16. Children's Bill of rights

Some say that children of family court are the victims of a divorce like victims of crime through no fault of their own. And a system that protects criminals with right to counsel but not truly innocent parents victimizes these children. Hence the need for children's Bill of rights.

Contributors are being sought to collaborate on a Children's Bill of Rights for next generation safety in children safety files for divorce court. But when look at children of divorce court in parallel with crime victims, then we can see that their safety hinges on the same basic human needs.

ILLINOIS CRIME VICTIMS

Bill of Rights

The Illinois Constitution and Illinois statutes provide that victims of violent crimes have the following rights:

- The right to be treated with fairness and respect for their dignity and privacy and to be free from harassment, intimidation and abuse throughout the criminal justice process.

- The right to notice of and to a hearing before a court ruling on a request for access to any of the victim's records, information or communications which are privileged or confidential by law.

- The right to timely notification of all court proceedings.

- The right to communicate with the prosecution.

- The right to be heard at any post-arraignment release decision, plea or sentencing.

- The right to be notified of the conviction, sentence, imprisonment and release of the accused.

- The right to timely disposition of the case following the arrest of the accused.

- The right to be reasonably protected from the accused throughout the criminal justice process.

- The right to have the safety of the victim and the victims family considered in denying or fixing the amount of bail, determining whether to release the defendant and setting conditions of release after arrest and conviction.

- The right to be present at trial and all other court proceedings on the same basis as the accused, unless the victim is to testify and the court determines that the victim's testimony would be materially affected if the victim hears other testimony at the trial.

- The right to have present at all court proceedings, subject to the rules of evidence, an advocate or other support person of the victim's choice.

- The right to restitution.

These rights are said by the Illinois Attorney General's website to apply in any adult criminal proceeding. Violent crimes listed include kidnapping, homicide, felony assaults and batteries, domestic battery, sexual assault, arson, driving under the influence, stalking, orders of protection violations, civil no contact orders, etc.

The law requires that these rights must be requested in writing when charges have been filed against an accused in the local state's attorney's office via "Notice of Victim's Assertion of Rights."

ILLINOIS DIVORCE VICTIMS

Bill of Rights

The Constitution and statutes of the future should provide that children of violent family law void monsters with at least the following rights:

- The right to be seen by family law 2.0 (aka micro justice).

- The right to be heard by micro justice.

- The right to be valued by micro justice.

- The right to have bridges built over official voids.

- The right to be treated with fairness and respect for their dignity and to be free from harassment, intimidation and abuse throughout the family justice process.

- The right to communicate with contemporary parents.

- The right to have a plug and play safety file at any negotiation, hearing, decision, discussion, or ruling.

- The right to be reasonably safe from voids throughout the family justice process.

- The right to have present at all court proceedings, subject to the rules of evidence, a united parent or other support person of the children's choice.

- The right to restitution from reckless and excessive void monsters.

17. Fertilizer –

The Fair Deal Standards Bill

Back Story to the Fair Dealing Standards Bill

We find these truth to be self-evident;
That all children are created equal.
That they are endowed by their Creator;
With right to safety bridges over voids;
That those bridges lead to life, liberty and the pursuit of happiness.
And without those bridges, death, bondage and draining despair.
What if tomorrow's leaders cared about children of divorce as much as other children?

Endowed Chair Dr. Brené Brown of the University of Houston says on the Oprah Winfrey website that, "I define connection as the energy that exists between people when they feel seen, heard, and valued..."

Fair Dealing Standards would finally mean that children could be seen, heard, and valued by the authors of their lives during the negotiations in divorce courts by placing an age restriction before they can be allowed in.

Fair Dealing Standards would open the door to a new chapter in America. A new chapter where children are treated like human beings and no longer treated alongside property in the terms of those divorce court contracts.

Fair Dealing Standards would exponentially reduce the amount of pain and suffering that these children endure in the short-term. And in the long-term Fair Dealing Standards would benefit society because these children would then grow up knowing that they are valued and not meant to fall through the cracks.

As classical divorce court "fighting file" gets thicker and thicker over years and years, then the more and more that children are torn and know the feeling of being left out to fall by the authors of their lives. As their entire lives are being diced up on the chopping block like a tomato, these unrepresented children feel more and more isolated, more and more unseen, more and more pressed, more and more unheard, more and more misplaced, more and more unvalued. No matter how they look, they're never seen by the authors of their lives. No matter how loud they cry, they're never heard. No matter how much pain they feel, they'll never given even a band aid. In fact, the longer and the thicker that these divorce court "fighting files" become, the more shushed and the more pain that children endure. This is the poisonous bite of unfair dealings.

The Fair Dealing Standards Bill would protect children in this device by adding age limits before they can enter. Then, children could be placed in the state-of-the-art child safety files which move hand-in-hand with fighting files. After all, we put bike lanes next to car lanes. We put child safety seats next to adult car seats. We even put happy meals next to value meals. So. why not child safety files next to fighting files? That's a no-brainer.

Since children are old enough to drive a car on the road between the ditches by the age of 16, then they are able to float during a swampy divorce by the time that they reach the age of 16. 14 for amicable divorces.

Fair Dealing Standards would protect the most vulnerable children in our society by not allowing them to be a part of divorce court contracts, or in the supervoid of the "double diabolical super divisive psychological warfare machine," until they reach the age of either 14 for an amicable divorce, or the age of 16 for a contentious divorce. Many adults are not equipped to survive the unfair dealing standards in state family court.

If anyone believes that state family courts are safe and humane for children, then they can take the Void Challenge. Be the unseen, unheard, unvalued, table-less, chair-less, unrepresented, partiless (as in Plaintiff, Defendant, etc.), and ungraded term of two opposing fighting parties. These voids are hidden dangers that only these children face.

Or, anyone can take the Void Challenge another way. If a child goes to kindergarten and never has a teacher, is never seen, never heard, and is never graded, then we can understand their chances of graduating.

Why don't we just leave kids out of school like family court, and just hire teachers?

Or, anyone can take the Void Challenge when they are sick by having two other people go to the doctors and a third doctor can decide which of those two doctors are correct to see how long it takes them personally to get well.

Why don't we just leave people out of hospitals, and just hire doctors?

Or, when you are discouraged, then two other people can go to a counselor and get cases started and a third counselor can ping-pong as hard as they can those two counselors around and around back and forth to see how long it takes you to get better.

Why should children have a safe place in the division equation?

Or, if an egg is on a nest, then another hen and another rooster can go to a third chicken and ping-pong the hen and rooster back and forth until one of them drops out to see how long it takes for the egg to hatch. Do you see the problem growing up in and after these voids?

Fair Dealing Standards would enable these children to float along safely through life while their Titanic of mom and dad bounce around and around back and forth into each other and through ice burgs.

Because children are always fragile, parents deserve to float, and there's no line between justice and injustice in state family courts. Please contact your US Congress member and ask them to support a Fair Dealing Standards Bill.

Children have always been involved in the separation of their parents. This is nothing new. But due to the convenience of "no-fault" divorce and the industrialization of those separations to the maximum since the late 20th century, the nature of these experiences has changed. For children, it went from something that grown-ups can help them handle to a severely divisive diabolical psychological warfare machine that no grown adult can safely navigate alone. This isn't all children, but Fair dealing Standards would not let any child go there.

Many groups have developed recently for their safety. They claim that a divorce should be handled more like a surgery than a mud throwing contest. Truly innocent parents and children at CLU (www.cleanlawunion.com) in Decatur, IL say that being unrepresented due to financial constraints when another parent is represented feels like being in an open void underneath of a waterfall for as long as the case is open and then beyond.

Children must feel like being in two open voids underneath of two waterfalls for as long as state family divorce cases are open and beyond. And US Census statistics confirm that these children are almost three times as likely to have educational issues, behavioral problems, early teen pregnancies, imprisonments, etc.

There was a time when children were abused as factory workers in America and sometimes worked 70 hours a week with no mandatory breaks. It took decades to outlaw child labor. It was not easy and did not have as many safety groups in place to prove what was going on as those for children of state family court do today.

By 1899, 28 states had passed legislation to regulate child labor. And many attempts were made to pass federal child labor laws. The US Congress passed two laws, in 1918 and 1922, but the Supreme Court deemed both of them unconstitutional. In 1924, Congress proposed a constitutional amendment against child labor, but the states did not ratify it.

Then, in 1938, Congress passed the Fair Labor Standards Act. It fixed a minimum age of 16 for children to be able to work during school days, 14 for certain jobs after school, and 18 for dangerous work. Similar standards exist for children being inside of an automotive vehicle. The family court vehicle can be disastrous. Especially without monitoring those children inside of it.

Today all states and the US government have regulations on child labor. These regulations for the most part have civilized the evils of children working in factories.

There should be an age limit for child in state family court cases in order to protect them from recklessly divisive inhumane treatment. There should be an age limit before children can enter in as the terms of a divorce court contract. Where they can be unconscionably used as leverage back and forth like property. It is currently free to barter time with children by trickery, false accusations, fraudulent orders of protection, gaming, spinning, twisting the facts, negotiating like for a car by kicking the tires, and then being written into terms of those deals likewise without being seen, heard, or valued. A Fair Dealing Standards Bill would open the door for the true scientific breakthrough of child safety files for the county who pioneers this movement.

CLU BRIDGE

System Safety

www.cleanlawunion.com

Acknowledgements

Graphic fonts by cooltext.com

Void monster graphics by BenDx

"For nothing is hidden,
except to be revealed;
nor has anything been secret,
but that it would come to light."

{Jesus in Mark 4:22}

www.ingramcontent.com/pod-product-compliance
Lightning Source LLC
Chambersburg PA
CBHW081255040426
42452CB00014B/2516